MW00632906

UNDERSTANDING AND ADDRESSING
ADOLESCENT
Grief Issues

UNDERSTANDING AND ADDRESSING
ADOLESCENT
Grief Issues

DAVID A. OPALEWSKI, M.A.
contributions by JOEL ROBERTSON, PHARM.D.

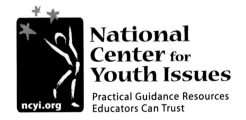

**National
Center for
Youth Issues**
Practical Guidance Resources
Educators Can Trust

P.O. Box 22185 • Chattanooga, TN 37422-2185
423.899.5714 • 800.477.8277
fax:423.899.4547 • www.ncyi.org

Duplication and Copyright

No part of this publication may be reproduced, stored in a retrieval system or transmitted in any form by any means, electronic, mechanical, photocopy , recording or otherwise without prior written permission from the publisher except for all worksheets and activities which may be reproduced for a specific group or class. Reproduction for an entire school or school district is prohibited.

P.O. Box 22185
Chattanooga, TN 37422-2185
423.899.5714 • 800.477.8277
fax: 423.899.4547
www.ncyi.org

ISBN: 978-1-931636-46-9
© 2007 National Center for Youth Issues, Chattanooga, TN
All rights reserved.

Written by: Dave Opalewski, M.A.
Contributions by: Joel C. Robertson, PHARM.D
Cover Design: Phillip Rodgers
Page Layout, design & contributing photography: Jacquelyn Kobet
Published by: National Center for Youth Issues

Printed in the United States of America

Table of Contents

About the Author

Dave Opalewski

Dave is president of Grief Recovery Inc., in Saginaw, Michigan, a consultant and co-author of "Confronting Death in the School Family," (published by the National Center for Youth Issues) "Teen Suicide Prevention for Schools and Communities," and author of "Guiding the Grieving Child." He has been a professional educator since 1972, working at the elementary, middle, high school, and college levels. Dave has been published several times in professional journals on the state and national levels.
He can be reached at:

Phone: 989-249-4362

Fax: 989-249-4363

Email: griefrecovery@chartermi.net

Forward

"A difficult age." "The awkward period." "Raging Hormones." "The age of many varied mood swings." Such quotes we have often heard concerning adolescents in today's world. You may even have heard many others. Although at times, many of these quotes are true in an adolescent's life, adults must never use them as an excuse for not communicating with adolescents or showing them compassion, empathy and understanding during difficult times.

Adolescents are not supposed to die. They feel invincible. They expect themselves and their friends to live a long time. It's against all the norms of nature. It is not fair. It is not right. Although it should never happen, the harsh reality is that it does happen, and when it does, it is a terrible shock for the adolescent. This is a time when a caring, unassuming adult can make a positive difference in a young person by fostering growth and maturity. If it were offered as a course in life, none of us would sign up for it, but we can be better off for having had this experience when handled in a caring and compassionate manner.

The death of a parent can result in the adolescent experiencing adult depression, neurosis, suicide, and physical illness later in life. (Breier 1988, Osterweiss, Solomon and Green 1984) At the time of death, adolescents may exhibit immediate reactions of withdrawal, helplessness, guilt, lack of concentration, insomnia and/or eating disorders. (McIntrye 1987, Osterweiss, Solomon and Green 1984) Experts conclude, however, that in time, healthy accommodation can take place following the death of an adolescent's parent if circumstances are favorable; that is, if caring, understanding and compassionate adults are willing to take an active approach to enhance the grief process of the adolescent.

In dealing with adolescents, as with any other group, respect must be demonstrated by the caring adult. They are not children or adults. They make up a special group of grievers who deserve a special kind of care and consideration from the adults in their world. Many times, however, adults expect teens to grieve like they do and expect that "time will heal all." Because of these "adult" expectations, communication barriers arise, and the caring adult loses his or her effectiveness in guiding the adolescent through this emotionally turbulent time.

Although there are cases where clinical help is necessary, one of our most common fundamental beliefs about grief is that it is best handled outside of the psychologist's or psychiatrist's office. Ordinary people who care and have compassion for their fellow human beings play an extremely important role toward the healing process of the grieving person. Many adolescent referrals to professionals would never have to be made if adults would take more time to learn about some simple supportive fundamentals in guiding the adolescent through the grief process.

We will never have all the answers as to why things happen. We will never always know what to say. The adolescent in a grief crisis may not be able to communicate any feeling soon after the tragedy. Because of these factors, it is easy for the adult to withdraw or even make an immediate referral for the adolescent to professional counseling. Although professional counseling may help, our research and experiences clearly show that the adolescent, in most cases, prefers to talk to a trusted adult where they already have an established relationship. Also, it doesn't matter to most adolescents what profession (factory worker, custodian, teacher, secretary, etc.) this trusted adult may belong to, as long as they show empathy, caring and compassion. Our first response to a grieving teen should not be to simply make an appointment with a professional for them, but to listen, talk, and communicate with them about their issues.

As much as adults may wish to protect adolescents from the pain and sorrow that accompanies death, life's experiences will lead to these encounters. Statistics indicate that one of every six children will lose one parent through death before they reach the age of 18. (Van Dexter, 1986) These experiences influence the total lives of the adolescents – their academic pursuits in school, their social lives, their relationships with family and friends, and their emotional selves.

Although we will never always know what to do, we do know that when our hearts are right, most of our instincts about what to do or say will be helpful. We cannot give a cure but we can give care. This unique group of grievers needs a caring touch from a caring adult if they themselves are to become caring, emotionally mature adults.

"Understanding and Addressing Adolescent Grief Issues" is a work dedicated to helping the caring adult guide the adolescent through this turbulent time.

Chapter 1

Experiences and Observations

Chapter One
Experiences and Observations

In this chapter, we will attempt to share some of our experiences of working with adolescents struggling through the grief process. Please note that we use the word *"process"* because grief is a *process*, not an *event*. We feel that sharing our experiences is the most effective way to communicate tested techniques, as it is clear from our research that adolescent grief is an area in need of much more attention. Many of the studies that have been done in the area of adolescent grief have some inherent problems. (Wolfelt' "Healing the Bereaved Child") There are discrepancies among control groups and definition of terms, causing gray areas that further frustrate the efforts of counselors, educators, and caring adults.

Most deaths that adolescents' experience are sudden and untimely. A parent may die of a heart attack, a brother or sister may die of an aneurysm, a friend may complete a suicide or be killed in a car accident. The very nature of these deaths often causes the adolescent to feel a prolonged and heightened sense of confusion and uncertainty. They become emotionally wounded by events beyond their control. Loss of this *"control"* can and often is a very frightening experience. After the shock and numbness wear off, depression will usually set in.

From our clinical and educational experiences, we easily conclude that adults generally communicate two philosophies to grieving teens: adolesc*ents should grieve like adults,* and *time will heal all.* Nothing can be further from the truth! Most adolescents have not been exposed to the many life experiences of an adult; therefore, when tragedy occurs, the adolescent has fewer life lessons from which to draw comfort and support. The maturity and reasoning levels of an adolescent are usually not the same as an adult's. Grief is a unique experience for all people. It is a unique experience for every individual adult. We must then conclude that as adults, we are putting unfair expectations upon adolescents to grieve similarly to adults. Many adults do this without realizing it.

Although it is true that time heals, time alone is not enough to heal the deep emotional wounds inflicted by the death of a loved one. The assumption that time will heal all, without any or very few interventions, communicates to adolescents that adults are indifferent. The philosophy that "time heals all" is, in our eyes, a typical adult cop-out. Providing opportunities to explore and share feelings is crucial to the healing process. In a later chapter we will be more specific as to how to make this happen.

Adolescents are also extremely close to boyfriends, girlfriends and best friends. If one of these significant people should die, they need the opportunity to mourn. Many times, unfortunately, we have witnessed their grief being overlooked because society tends to focus on the "primary mourners" – the dead person's immediate family. Because of this oversight, it is very probable that this adolescent will perceive that his/her feelings are not important; therefore, their sorrow is not validated.

Here are some common practical errors adults make when interacting with a grieving teen:

Saying, "I know how you feel"

When we tell adolescents "I know how you feel," we are actually telling them that they can't talk to us because they know that we *don't* know how they feel. Since grief is a unique experience for every individual, it is impossible to know exactly what another grieving person is feeling. Past experiences, plus a host of other unique dynamics in a person's life, work together to form a singular grief experience for every individual.

Putting unrealistic responsibility on the adolescent

For example, a young adolescent's father just died in a car accident. A caring adult puts his arm around the boy shortly after the funeral and says, "*You have to be the man of the house now and take care of your mother and little sister.*" This young adolescent has just lost his father. He will usually wonder if he can care for himself let alone his mother or younger sister. The possibility of the adolescent having to be "the man of the house" is what the adolescent *doesn't* need.

Saying, "If you need me, call me"

This call rarely happens and, to be frankly honest, the person who offers the help knows that in most cases they will not get a call. Many times the grieving person is so consumed by his grief he either forgets the offer or is in too much pain to call. Because of this, the "caring" adult has taken himself off the hook. Therefore, in reality, the "*If you need me, call me*" statement is a cop-out. It communicates to adolescents that "we really would rather not get involved unless we have to." The adolescent, like the grieving adult, can draw this conclusion rather simply; you don't want to be involved in a situation that is depressing and painful.

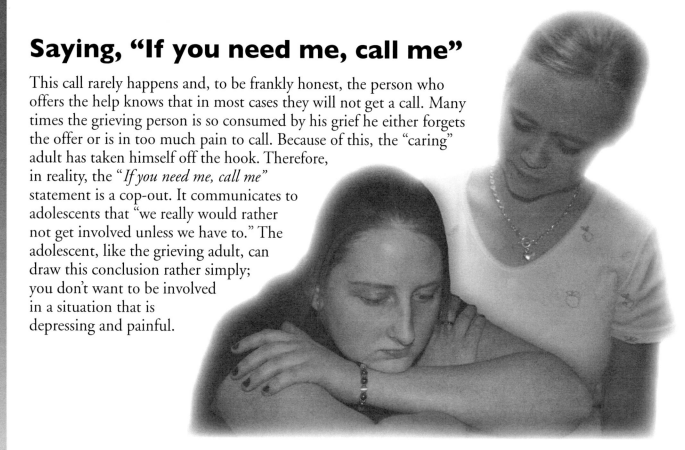

Minimizing the loss

"At least you still have your mother." "At least you still have other brothers and sisters." "At least you were expecting her to die." "At least he went quickly and didn't suffer." We have all too often heard these "well-meaning" statements made to grieving adolescents by "well-meaning" adults. We should *never* minimize the loss of a loved one to anybody. Since the adolescent is feeling very sad, the caring adult lays guilt upon the adolescent for feeling so sad. The adult who makes statements such as these communicates to the adolescent that they have absolutely no insight as to what they are going through and will obviously be of no help.

The list can go on and on; however, these are the most common mistakes that we have witnessed in our experiences. Please don't beat yourself up if you made some of these mistakes; however, please read on if you care to make a positive difference in the lives of adolescents grieving the loss of a loved one.

Chapter 2

Uniqueness of Adolescent Grief

Chapter Two
Uniqueness of Adolescent Grief

When a family experiences the death of one of its members, every member of that family has a great need to feel understood, yet has a natural incapacity to be understanding. A sensitive and caring adult can be a major support to the adolescent whose parent(s) are so consumed by their own grief that they just can't possibly reach out to comfort and support them.

As children pass to adolescence, studies clearly show that they take on adult perceptions of death. Death is seen as universal, but they see their own deaths far off in the future. (Matter & Matter 1982) The work of Lonetto and Templer in a 1986 study shows evidence that those early and middle-aged adult attitudes about mortality are very similar to the adolescent. However, in most cases, the similarity stops there.

Although adolescents are not as dependent as they were in childhood, their independence is still quite fragile. After the death of a friend or family member, they may feel helpless and frightened. Many want to retreat to childhood, where they felt a strong sense of protection. Societal expectations, however, compel them to behave like an adult. Many feel that they have to be strong to comfort family members, yet are still feeling frightened and helpless. As a result, the adolescent may be unable to share his or her feelings with anyone. Many may appear that they are coping quite well when, in fact, they are not. Real feelings are buried and not dealt with. These feelings will eventually come back from the depths to rear their ugly heads to inflict heavy emotional wounds upon the adolescent.

After the death of a friend or family member, teens can feel helpless and frightened. Many want to retreat to childhood, where they felt a strong sense of protection.

© National Center For Youth Issues • www.ncyi.org • 1-800-477-8277
Please refer to page 4 for duplication information

Anger is a common grief reaction of the adolescent. Anger gives the adolescent a sense of "power" to overcome the feelings of helplessness.

Anger

Anger is a common grief reaction of the adolescent. This anger gives the adolescent a sense of "power" to overcome the feelings of helplessness. The caring adult needs to encourage the adolescent to express anger in an acceptable way. Throwing chairs, punching walls, insulting people and other inappropriate behaviors are unacceptable methods of expression and tend to cause more complex problems for the adolescent as future conflicts enter into his life. In our support groups, we have rules about expressing anger in an appropriate manner and strongly believe that these rules have *not* inhibited adolescents in expressing how they feel. *(Sample support group rules, Chapter 10 p. 71)*

Denial

Denial is another common reaction of the adolescent to the death of a significant person in his life. Granger Westberg, in his book "Good Grief," says, "Denial is a common defense mechanism used to numb the intense pain a person is suffering from the shock of a terrible loss." This denial can be compared to a person going to the dentist to have a cavity filled. The dentist gives his patient a shot of novocaine. This temporary numbing prevents the patient from feeling the pain of the drill on his tooth. Denial temporarily shelters the adolescent from feeling this overwhelming pain all at once. If denial goes on for an extended period of time, however, the adolescent might be suffering from trauma and a referral to a mental health professional may be necessary. The caring adult must gently help the adolescent face the pain and move into the grief process. The adolescent may see grief as the problem. The caring adult must help the adolescent see that grief and the grief process is the solution to coming to grips with the loss.

Guilt

Guilt is many times a major problem with the adolescent. Adolescent guilt over the loss of a loved one can be unique from any other age group, especially if the death is the death of a parent. It is normal adolescent nature to question many of their parents' values. They question religion, beliefs about education, reasons for rules and guidelines set by parents, along with many other principles. Adolescents test adults to see if they are who they say they are. All this is a *normal part of the growing-up process.* The adolescent is experiencing his individuality. The adolescent who doesn't test or question parental values and philosophies of life is rare indeed, and may even be abnormal. If the death of a parent occurs during this time of testing, the adolescent usually feels a great deal of guilt. The adolescent looks upon himself as a bad kid who made life difficult for his deceased parent. This guilt is usually a barrier for the adolescent to enter into the grief process. As we have already stated, grief is the solution, not the problem. The caring adult must take the time to explain (not lecture) to the adolescent that the "testing time" is a normal phase of adolescence; he is not a bad person for going through this phase. In most cases, parents are aware of this phase, expect it to happen and accept it as a normal part of growing up. Parents also went through this phase when they were adolescents.

Making Sense of it All

The typical adolescent usually doesn't know how people are supposed to act and grieve. Although most adults would be hard pressed to describe and model "appropriate grief behavior," the lack of life experiences makes it even more awkward for the adolescent. Adolescents may see their friends each impacted a little differently than they are and become confused and uneasy about their own feelings and behaviors. The caring adult must explain to the adolescent that grief is a unique experience for every individual. Because of our natural human complexities and experiences, it is nearly impossible for two people to grieve exactly the same way. With this in mind, it is important for the caring adult to stress to the adolescent that he not place behavioral expectations upon his peers. The caring adult must help the adolescent realize that he will not feel the same way all the time during the grief process. He will have good times as well as bad. This is normal.

The ongoing task of being an adolescent usually does interfere with the grief process. Typical adolescent problems are: resistance and difficulty in communicating with adults, being overly concerned with acceptance by peers (especially if the death was a suicide), and friends who either don't know what to say or are afraid of saying the wrong thing, so they say nothing at all. It is very easy for the adolescent to perceive that his friends don't care. Alienation may take place. The adolescent then feels all alone to face emotional pain from not only the loss of the deceased, but also the loss of friends. With this perception of no help in sight, there is a strong chance depression will set in, making it even more difficult for the caring adult to reach this troubled adolescent.

Rage fantasies may also occur. This is a typical adolescent grief response, (especially if someone is clearly at fault), though most do not act on these feelings. The caring adult must help the adolescent to determine the difference between feeling rage and acting upon it and the subsequent consequences which may result from acting on that rage. The caring adult must help the adolescent find appropriate ways to express anger and rage.

In summary, adolescents have the same aspects of grief as adults do – anger, sadness, guilt, helplessness, fear – but they express them in ways appropriate to their stage of development. (Matter & Matter 1982) The caring adult will need to become familiar with these developmental stages so they can gain valuable insight into guiding the adolescent during this troubled time.

© National Center For Youth Issues • www.ncyi.org • 1-800-477-8277
Please refer to page 4 for duplication information

Chapter 3

Normal or Abnormal? Grief or Trauma?

Chapter Three

Normal or Abnormal? Grief or Trauma?

At the onset of the tragedy, it is very difficult to determine the normal grieving adolescent from the abnormal one. Our immediate goal is to show compassion, support and comfort and not to judge normal from the abnormal unless, of course, we feel the young person is in danger of harming himself and/or others. The abnormal usually shows up in extremes of intensity and duration. If an adolescent's grief is abnormal, it will usually show up with time. The following criteria will give the caring adult an inclination of whether the teen is grieving in a normal or abnormal manner:

Normal	Abnormal
Responds to comfort and support	Rejects comfort and support
Is often openly angry	Complains, is irritable, may not express anger
Will connect feelings with death	Do not relate feelings to any life event
Still can have enjoyable moments	Project a pervasive sense of doom
Sadness and emptiness are detected	Projects sense of hopelessness, emptiness
Expresses guilt over some aspect of loss	Usually generalized feelings of guilt
Self-esteem is temporarily impacted	Deep loss of self esteem

The assessment of normal versus abnormal grief behaviors usually has to be determined over a series of interactions between the caring adult and the grieving adolescent. Although it may be possible to determine immediately, this is not usually the case. One abnormal behavior listed above is reason to be concerned. The caring adult may wish to encourage professional counseling for the adolescent who either displays several of the abnormal behaviors or one of the abnormal behaviors for a prolonged period of time. Remember that death is a foreign concept to the teenager. The resulting grief can be even more confusing. This creates the great need for a caring adult to be willing to listen and comfort in this difficult time.

Death is a foreign concept to the teenager. The resulting grief can be even more confusing. This creates the great need for a caring adult to be willing to listen and give comfort.

Difference Between Grief and Trauma

At this point, we need to make a distinction between grief and trauma. Grief is the intense feeling that overwhelms an individual as a result of a tragic event in the individual's life. The word "trauma" is from the Greek root meaning "wound." Just as physical trauma may overwhelm the body's defenses and cause disability and chronic pain, psychological trauma may overwhelm the mind's defenses and cause lasting emotional harm. Trauma is an event that is outside the range of usual human experience and would be seriously distressing for almost anyone. Trauma knows no barriers, no distinction between age and cultures. Adolescents experiencing grief may not experience trauma; however, if they experience trauma they will experience grief. The differences between adolescents experiencing trauma and grief are as follows:

Grief	Trauma
Generalized reaction – Inconsolable	Generalized reaction – Panic
Behaviors generally known to public and professional	Behaviors largely unknown to public
Most can tell their story of tragedy	Most don't want to talk about tragedy
Anguish in acknowledgement of the loss	Anguish triggers panic, loss of control,
Animosity is generally non-destructive or assaultive	Animosity often becomes combative
Generally does not engage in self-destructive behaviors	High risk for self-destructive behaviors
Hindsight says "I wish I would/would not have	Hindsight says "It is my fault"
Dreams tend to be of deceased	Dreams are about self as victim

If the caring adult suspects that the adolescent is experiencing some form of trauma, a referral to a professional psychological clinic would be appropriate. Because of age, the adolescent would, in most cases, need parental permission for treatment.

The professional's goals for the adolescent at this time may include the following:

- Get the adolescent to normal functioning as quickly as possible.
- Help the adolescent gain some sense of control.
- Help the adolescent re-establish their sense of equilibrium.

Even though a referral is made and followed through, the caring adult still has a major role in caring for the grieving adolescent. The caring adult needs to stay in touch with the adolescent. The major goals at this time are:

- Maintaining a friendly relationship to help the adolescent re-establish a sense of "trusting adult" connection to the world.
- Helping the adolescent regain hope.

Too often in this world, when an adolescent is referred for professional treatment, we think the problem is no longer ours. Research clearly points out, however, that the grieving adolescent is best served by a team of coordinated treatment and support by caring adults in his life.

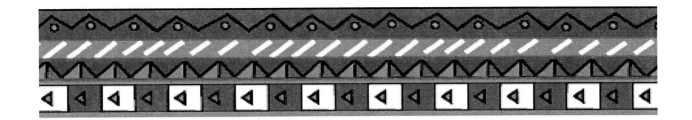

Remember the African proverb,

"It takes
a *village*
to *raise*
a child."

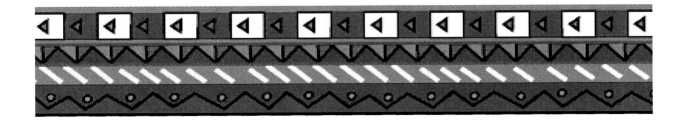

Chapter 4

Sudden Death Versus Anticipated Death

Chapter Four
Sudden Death Versus Anticipated Death

Is there a difference in the grieving process if the adolescent experiences an anticipated death as opposed to a tragedy involving a sudden death? Although grief is grief any way you look at it, the process of grieving is much different when experiencing a sudden death compared to anticipated death. In no way are we suggesting that any one experience is harder or easier than the other. Both experiences are tough. People, however, often de-value a person's grief when they say things like "at least you were expecting it" (anticipated) or "at least he didn't have to suffer" (sudden). When anyone says things like this, they usually take themselves totally out of the picture for helping the grieving adolescent.

So What Is the Difference?

There are different dynamics in each situation that affect the grief process. The grief process in an anticipated death starts for the family while the dying person is still living. The shock, numbness, denial and guilt phases of the grief cycle are usually present for family members as they work to cope with the situation. The greatest time of need for these grievers is while the person is lingering and, of course, at the time of death. However, for most grievers, at the time of death, they are well along into the grief process, although a slide back to the beginning grief stages is normal for a shorter period of time.

Relief or Guilt?

Usually, if the deceased suffered while lingering, the surviving loved ones will feel relief. The caring adult must be aware that the survivor may at some future point feel guilty for feeling relieved at the time of their loved one's death. This may occur as long as six months after the death. This is normal. The caring adult may help the grieving adolescent to see that the suffering of their loved one caused them great pain and anguish. To feel relief from this situation is normal and healthy. The caring adult must reassure the grieving adolescent that he is not a bad person for feeling relief at the time of his loved one's death, and that many other people have had similar feelings. Because the grieving adolescent starts the grief process while their loved one is lingering, they usually "recover" sooner than does a person who suffers the sudden death of a loved one. Although we should never tell people how or what to feel, the caring adult may comfort by asking the questions on the following page. Copy and use the form on the following page as you talk to grieving teens.

> # People often *de-value*
> # a person's grief when they say things like
> # "at least you were expecting it" *(anticipated)*
> # or "at least he didn't have to suffer." *(sudden)*

Relief or Guilt Inventory Worksheet

1. Why do you feel guilty? _____

_____

_____

_____

_____

_____

_____

2. Is your guilt realistic in light of the suffering and pain your loved one experienced?

_____

_____

_____

_____

_____

_____

_____

3. Would you want him back the way he was the last few months of his life?

_____

_____

_____

_____

_____

_____

_____

Denial

For the adolescent who experiences the sudden death of a loved one, the process of denial is much more severe. Denial may last long after the funeral. During the funeral process, many grievers are not aware of the situation or don't accept what happened. This denial becomes a stumbling block for the grieving person as they begin the grief process.

Anger or Revenge?

Those who experience the sudden death of a loved one are often angry. This anger is either internalized or vented at family members or close friends. In the case of an innocent person dying because of a drunk driver, the survivors are often livid. Although we can understand the reason for them feeling so, they make the common mistake of focusing on catching and punishing the guilty person. This anger and revenge, or as we call it "rage fantasy," will prevent the grieving person from entering into the grief work they must do if healing is to occur.

Feelings of anger or revenge can be refocused by doing the following:

About one month after the funeral, help the adolescent make a genuine effort to focus on the person who died and not the cause of death. What happened cannot be changed, so we must press on the best we can. To accomplish this goal, the caring adult can do two things:

- Help the teen focus on the good memories of the deceased. Someone once said, "a person is not really dead until they are forgotten." Although we may disagree about this person's definition of death, he has a good point in not forgetting the person who died. Great comfort can be found in the fond memories.

- Help the adolescent concentrate on the legacy of the dead person. Focusing on the legacy can give reason for hope and the assurance that the deceased person's life was not in vain. It also can give the adolescent an appreciation of life and of his living loved ones.

- Guide the teen to use their energy to do something positive in their loved one's memory.

    A. Organize a fund-raiser walk, etc. in their honor and give proceeds to an organization that supports a special cause. (**MADD**)

    B. Make a memory quilt about their life and display it or keep it as a comfort to themselves.

    C. Organize a balloon release with thoughts of the loved one attached to the string.

> ## In guiding the adolescent through the sudden death of a loved one, the caring adult must remember that *grief is not the problem, it is the solution.* Help the adolescent focus away from the cause of death and focus on happier memories of the deceased loved one.

The Spiritual Aspect

Although our spiritual lives can be a major pillar on which to lean, many times while trying to explain or understand the spiritual aspect, we can get out of balance and confused. Religious beliefs can and are a source of great strength. However, those who are religious are not immune to pain. Religious and non-religious people alike must go through the grief process. It is important for the caring adult to be sensitive to the religious beliefs of the grieving adolescent and not to push personal religious beliefs on them. It is our experience that in the midst of intense emotional pain brought on by grief, especially soon after a death has occurred, is not the time for philosophical religious debates. Although we have strong convictions regarding the importance and benefits of spiritual values, the grieving adolescent's greatest need at the time of tragedy is to be listened to, not to have Bible verses quoted to him.

The following comments have been frequently heard in our adolescent grief support groups:

"I should be happy; She is in Heaven."

The grieving person who makes this statement is actually telling us that she is in a sorrowful mood. To make things worse, the grieving person also is probably feeling guilty for feeling sad. The caring adult needs to stress to the grieving adolescent the following grief principle; "We don't grieve for the person who died; we grieve for ourselves and our loss." Even though the deceased person may be in heaven, she is still missed by her loved ones. Many of our adolescents in our grief support groups report being told that "they should be happy because their deceased loved ones are in heaven." All of these adolescents have stated to us they sense a great deal of guilt is being heaped on them for feeling this way. Although this statement may be made by a well-meaning adult, it usually has very little, if any comforting effect.

"If my faith were stronger, I wouldn't be sad."

Having a strong religious faith, no matter what faith or what the religion looks like, does not give emotional immunity to the grieving person. A casual student of biblical history can name a large number of biblical characters with great faith who grieved the death of loved ones. Jesus Christ cried at the death of Lazarus. People of faith are not immune to pain, including emotional pain. *Religious beliefs give hope, but they are not pain killers.*

"I am supposed to be strong, my religious faith says so."

It is sometimes true that a grieving person has to be strong for surviving family members; however, there comes a time when they too have to grieve. Hopefully, this "time of strength" will be a short period of time, because in order to heal, we must grieve. When a grieving adolescent feels this way, the caring adult must encourage them to grieve and stress the importance of working through the grief process. In some cases, the adult needs to give the young person permission to grieve.

Religious and non-religious persons alike must go through the grief process. Grief is not the problem, it is the solution.

Chapter 5

Adolescent Suicide

Chapter Five

Adolescent Suicide

As we have studied adolescent suicide statistics published by The Center for Disease Control (CDC) in Atlanta the past ten years, we've see that suicide has been the fastest growing killer of American youth. It is very difficult to know actual numbers as experts claim several suicides are actually reported as accidents because of "inconclusive evidence." When the evidence casts a small shadow of doubt, the incident is usually reported as an accident. The CDC lists suicide as the third leading cause of death in adolescents; however, when we factor in even a small percentage of the above-mentioned "accidents," a strong argument exists as suicide actually being the second leading cause of death for American youth.

Some compelling statistics concerning adolescent suicide include:

- Up to 60% of American high school students report having suicide ideation.
  (Mich. Assoc. of Suicidology 2004)

- Suicide has increased 124% in American middle schools from 1994 to 2004.
  (CDC, 2004)

- Within a typical classroom, it is likely that three students (one boy and two girls) have made a serious suicide attempt in the last year.
  (Mich. Assoc. of Suicidology, 1999)

- Each completed suicide dramatically impacts 6 other adolescents, not including classmates.

- In the year 2000, 3,994 adolescents killed themselves *(Granello & Granello, 2006)*

- Estimates range from 50 to 200 suicide attempts for every completed suicide.
  (McEvoy & McEvoy 1994)

Up to 60% of American high school students report having suicide ideation. (Mich. Assoc. of Suicidology 2004)

From this list we can see the magnitude of the problem, and the disturbing statistics go on and on. The intent of this chapter is to help adults care for and guide adolescents affected by the suicide of another.

There is no doubt that suicide compounds the already difficult grief process. Some differences in the grief process between grief from suicide and grief from death other than suicide include:

Survivors often see suicide as rejection.

They may feel that the person who completed the suicide did not care about them, their feelings and their friendship.

Suicide deaths tend to be more violent and gruesome.

The adolescent usually experiences trauma, especially if he found the deceased. Unless this trauma is treated, the grief process will most likely come to a standstill. Survivors usually need to restate many times over what they saw, heard, smelled, etc. The caring adult must be patient. It may take several repeats for the survivor to process the experience.

Society attaches taboo, shame, and blame to suicide.

Ostracism is all too common for the adolescent grieving a suicidal death of a family member. Many grieving teens affected by suicide report being avoided by friends, teachers neighbors. Adolescents who have experienced a suicide in their families report losing friends because their friends' parents won't let them associate together. The point we must make to the friends of the survivor is not to be judgmental. Suicides occur in all kinds of families. The survivors don't need us to judge them or their families. They need us to comfort, support and guide them. The question we need to ask ourselves is, "Who are we to judge?"

Friends and family often blame themselves for not stopping the suicide.

Blame either directed at themselves or others is unhealthy. The caring adult needs to impress upon the adolescent that it was the deceased's decision to complete suicide, not theirs or anyone else's.

Experiencing Guilt

Adolescents may experience guilt about not seeing the signs or not being able to help when behavioral clues manifested. We call this the "I could have, should have, would have syndrome" (although no such syndrome has been published). Much of this guilt is unfounded. The friends of the completer were his friends, not his doctor or counselor. Our advice to the caring adult is to guide (not lecture or preach to) the young person through these thoughts, helping them to arrive at appropriate, healthy clarifications of them.

Anger toward the person who committed suicide is common.

Many survivors display anger toward the person who died. Many survivors are especially enraged by their certainty that the one who took his life wanted to cause them pain or had no consideration for their feelings. The truth of the matter is that suicidal people are in so much inner pain and turmoil, it is practically impossible for them to focus on how their suicide will impact others. The suicidal person is in a state of depression which interferes with rational thinking. It is also a well known fact that depression is a medical condition, not necessarily the result of character flaws. When survivors come to an understanding of these facts, it is easier to deal with and alleviate their anger.

Pitfalls of the Healing Process

Healing after the suicide of a significant person in the life of an adolescent is a long and difficult process. It is important for the caring adult to be aware of the following difficulties that may be encountered during the healing process:

- **Anniversary reactions** – Yearly, monthly and even the weekly anniversaries of the death are frequent stimuli for depression. Anniversaries of the event bring about the painful awareness that the loved one is gone.

- **A feeling that nothing else matters** – There is a tendency to blame all of their unhappiness on the suicide. It becomes a convenient excuse for not having to deal with other problems.

- **Substance Abuse** – Hiding from the pain will not bring about growth and healing. Remember, grief is not the problem, it is the solution. Unfortunately, we have to hurt to heal. Postponing the pain prolongs and may even complicate the grief process.

- **Ignoring one's own health** – During the shock, it is common for the adolescent to neglect his own well being. Sleep disturbance and loss of appetite cause the body to become run down. The adolescent is especially vulnerable to physical illness.

- **Milestones** – Normal changes that occur may also reverse the progress being made toward recovery. Change is associated with growth and loss. Graduations, prom and other important milestones mean moving on to something new while giving up something in the past. Each new step in the teen's life moves him away from the experiences he shared with the deceased.

Moving towards healing

The old adage "time heals all wounds" is not necessarily true for survivors of suicide. Although time is necessary for healing, time alone is not enough. Sharing of feelings with family members, friends, caring adults, counselors, pastors and others is vital to healing the pain of a loved one's suicide. Adult support by listening, understanding, non-judgmental mentoring and the skillful rebuilding of the adolescent's self-esteem are essential to a healing outcome. The principles in our chapter, *"Basics for the Caring Adult" (Chapter 7 p. 51-53)* will be very helpful in working with adolescents grieving the suicide of a loved one.

Suicidal people are in so much inner pain and turmoil, it is practically impossible for them to focus on how their suicide will impact others.

Chapter
6

Common Adolescent Grief Concerns

Chapter Six
Common Adolescent Grief Concerns

In our many years of experience working with adolescents dealing with grief and bereavement issues, and also from scouring the literature, we have identified twelve common issues associated with grieving youth. The following is a list of these concerns followed by suggestions we hope the caring adult will find helpful:

The intensity of pain felt

Most adolescents are surprised by the intensity of pain. Most will feel that this is abnormal. The caring adult can explain to the adolescent that they have been emotionally wounded. Grief cuts emotions like a knife cuts flesh. Both hurt and leave scars; however, with help from the caring adult, they do heal.

Concerns about numbness

Often teens experiencing grief can't feel anything, which may lead to confusion as they see others grieving openly. The caring adult can comfort the young person by pointing out that this numbness is a normal grief reaction. Numbness is a natural body defense mechanism that protects people from feeling overloaded with pain. The caring adult must encourage the adolescent to let his emotions out when he is ready.

Comparing personal grief to others'

It is of paramount importance that the caring adult point out to the adolescent that no two people grieve alike. Grief is a unique experience for every individual. The grieving adolescent is not fair to himself when he compares his method of grieving to that of others. There is no set timetable for grief. People cannot and should not judge their grieving process by comparing it to others'.

How long will my grief last?

Teens, as well as adults, are usually unaware of the length of a normal grief cycle. The caring adult needs to stress that dealing with death takes time. According to experts, the grief cycle may last as long as two years; however, rarely will the adolescent be upset every day for two years. The sadness may come and go during that time. The cycle may repeat itself during a person's life, depending on individual experiences and a host of many present and future dynamics that transpire in the person's life. As previously mentioned, there is no set timetable for grief.

The caring adult must encourage the adolescent to let his emotions out when he is ready.

Is it wrong to have fun?

The caring adult can respond to the adolescent by impressing upon him that he has a right and responsibility to enjoy life, even if a friend or family member is gone. Although he will have sad times, he is entitled to laugh and have fun when he is in the mood.

How should I act?

When adolescents are out of their comfort zone, especially as a result of a tragedy, their anxiety increases. The caring adult should stress that there is no single appropriate way to respond to death, as grief is a unique experience to all people. Some people may cry, some are quiet. Just because people are quiet doesn't mean that they are not hurting. They may be crying inside. The caring adult should gently and skillfully help the adolescent turn his focus to his own personal feelings and respect the feelings and expressions (or lack of) of others.

Why do I feel so sad when I hardly knew the person who died?

This is a valid concern of adolescents which needs to be addressed. Many times, we have witnessed adults who will make the mistake of judging an adolescent's intensity of grief because they hardly knew the deceased. They can, and in many cases do, feel the pain of grief. They may be reminded of sad experiences in their life or may be frightened that they too, could die. Even the death of an acquaintance can be a frightening experience for an adolescent.

What is normal?

This is a very difficult question indeed because what is "normal" can be different for many people, based on their different experiences and backgrounds. The caring adult should encourage the adolescent not to compare his grief to that of another person. We all hurt and have a right to express it in our own special *appropriate* manner. ***Review pages 25 and 26 to help determine when grief may be something more serious that requires professional attention***.

The "cocooning" syndrome

Many adolescents are afraid to get close to someone else after they have experienced the death of a close friend. They may have the fear of that person dying too, or they may feel that they are betraying their deceased friend. Whatever the reason, the caring adult must try to impress on the young person that isolating himself will only make him lonelier. It is unlikely that another close friend would die; however, there is no guarantee that it won't happen. Reaching out to friends, however, can lessen the pain and help tremendously through this difficult time. Also, needing a friend at this time can be a tribute to the friend who died. This deceased friend obviously helped the grieving teen realize the importance of friendship.

A changing circle of friends

This common dynamic for grieving adolescents can cause the young person to feel that he is losing more than his deceased friend. Adults should explain that some of the grieving adolescent's friends may need to break away from the painful reminders of the friend they lost, which may include friends they shared in common. This, many times, is temporary. The teen should be encouraged to open up and talk to other people and make new friends. They should also know that as time goes on, they may find themselves returning to their old circle of friends. Many teens in our grief support groups report that when this happens, the friendships tend to be much deeper and stronger than they were before the tragedy.

When adolescents are out of their comfort zone, especially as a result of tragedy, their anxiety increases. Stress that there is no single appropriate way to respond to death, as grief is a unique experience to all people.

The "smothering parent" syndrome

The caring adult needs to communicate to the adolescent that it is okay for him to want some space and that he need not feel guilty about wanting his parents to know that he needs a little space. However, advise the adolescent to do so *kindly*. In defending the parent, the adult might say, "Your friend's death scared your parents too. They may be afraid of losing you." The caring adult may also encourage the adolescent to say things like, "I need to deal with this. Please don't try to protect me." Also, "Please don't tell me how to feel. When I talk to you about my feelings, I'd appreciate if you would just listen. If I want to talk to another adult – a teacher, counselor or minister – it doesn't mean that I am rejecting you. I just want to talk to someone who isn't so close to me." The caring adult should try to defend the parent, but validate the young person's feelings, giving them some concrete things to consider, while communicating to his parents.

The "something must be wrong with me if I need to see a counselor" syndrome

Many adolescents feel that something is wrong with them if they feel a need to talk to a professional counselor or psychologist. The caring adult needs to communicate to them that speaking to a professional counselor or psychologist is no different than going to a medical doctor when you are physically sick. Tell them directly that "if you need to speak to such a person after someone close to you has died, you are *not* sick. You have been injured by events beyond your control, and you need help for your injury." Although adolescents may have other concerns, we believe that it will help caring adults aid teens dealing with grief. We cannot give a cure, but we can give care. Empathy, warmth and acceptance are essential qualities as the caring adult attempts to help the adolescent understand the loss and grow to be an emotionally healthy adult.

© National Center For Youth Issues • www.ncyi.org • 1-800-477-8277
Please refer to page 4 for duplication information

Chapter 7

Basics for the Caring Adult

Chapter Seven

Basics for the Caring Adult

The caring adult must understand that he cannot "fix" the grief situation for the adolescent or help them "get over" their grief. Grief is a situation you never get over, but you must go through. Adolescents, like all people, never overcome grief; they live with it and work to reconcile themselves to it. The caring adult, however, can be an important and vital resource in helping the adolescent to come to grips with his grief. The following is a list of "basic fundamentals" to help the caring adult guide young people in this troubled time.

Put yourself in their shoes

Empathy is an essential quality for the caring adult as he works with the teen; empathy *with* the adolescent, not *for* the adolescent. When we give empathy, we give companionship. To give empathy, the caring adult must develop the capacity to project himself into the adolescent's world and to view the situation through their eyes. It also means the adult must make an effort to understand the meaning of the teen's grief experience without imposing his own meaning on the adolescent's experience from the outside. Empathy does not involve the direct expression of one's feelings but focuses on the feelings of the other. Empathy picks up where sympathy leaves off. It helps to develop a close, trusting and meaningful relationship. Being empathetic does not mean that the caring adult passively waits for the grieving adolescent to say something. The caring adult has to be actively, as well as attentively, involved as feelings are explored and expressed in order to attempt to grasp what the adolescent feels inside. What are the unique meanings of loss to the teen? What is he trying to express that he just can't say? The caring adult must expand his own boundaries to include those of the adolescent he is caring for.

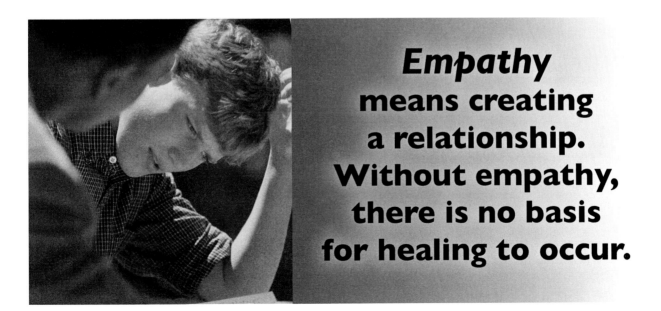

Empathy **means creating a relationship. Without empathy, there is no basis for healing to occur.**

Get to know them and understand from their perspective

While empathy is of extreme importance in working with the grieving adolescent, it in and of itself is not enough. The caring adult must be able to communicate this sense of understanding (gained through empathy) to the young person. This ability to communicate understanding helps the adolescent feel secure, trusted and affirmed. Also, the more the caring adult is willing to let the grieving adolescent teach him, the more he will be able to understand. A genuine commitment on the part of the caring adult to understand creates a trusting, less threatening environment for the youth.

This environment is conducive to honest and healthy expression of feelings. Although the caring adult will never be able to understand all of their feelings, the adolescent will usually sense the adult's desire and effort to understand. Eye contact from the adult to the teen is another important factor in communicating the desire to understand. Talking to the adolescent without eye contact may convey, "I'm tired of talking to you about this" or "I don't have much time, so let's get this over with." This situation may then communicate to the adolescent a feeling of rejection. This feeling of rejection may close the door to any future discussions which may prove beneficial to the adolescent.

Compassion

The caring adult communicates sensitivity and warmth by trying to put himself in the grieving adolescent's situation. If the caring adult can be sensitive to the young person's unique perspective, he stands a good chance to see his natural anxieties. In other words, the adult must concern himself with the teen's perception of the situation, not his own or that of the community. For instance, if an adolescent's mother completed a suicide, the adolescent may perceive this as rejection by the mother. The caring adult must be able to sense what the adolescent is thinking and feeling. Sensitivity and warmth implies patience, caring and the ability to hear and respond to the grieving teen's needs.

Acceptance

At the time of loss, the caring adult must understand that the goal is to understand the adolescent's feelings and assist, not judge, the adolescent or his behavior. To communicate acceptance, the caring adult must expect that some questions might seem shocking or irrelevant. The adult must respond to such questions without shock or embarrassment so the adolescent will feel respected. Acceptance is also about never hurting the adolescent's self-esteem. The caring adult must be willing to accept them not only for what they are, but also for what they are capable of becoming.

Trust

Trust is another very integral quality in working with adolescents in painful situations such as grieving the loss of a close friend or loved one. Adolescents often feel a lack of trust in their world because of the death of a friend or loved one. They often wonder if they should risk loving and making close friendships again. The adolescent must learn over time that he can trust again. When tragic experiences have influenced the adolescent's world, trust can be difficult for the caring adult to achieve, unless an established relationship already exists between the adolescent and adult.

To cultivate trust, the caring adult must stay consistent with words and behaviors. If the adult sets a time for a meeting, he should be on time. Also, the caring adult must follow through on all promises he may make to the grieving adolescent. For the most part, trust is about being consistent and providing a safe atmosphere that allows for honest expression of thoughts and feelings. The caring adult must help the grieving adolescent feel consistently safe.

Flexibility

In all of the years of experience we have working with youth, we have come to the conclusion that flexibility is a vital characteristic for being effective in working with grieving adolescents. Grief counseling is not like teaching with a lesson plan. Since grief is a unique experience for all, no lesson plans exist for the many unique situations that will arise.

The caring adult must learn to respond to the ever changing, moment-to-moment situation as he sees it. By responding with spontaneity, the adult is able to address the unique needs of the moment. Our advice to the caring adult who may feel a bit frightened about this is, "Say what feels right." We have found that when your heart is right, so will be most of your responses. The more we work with adolescents, the more we have learned how important it is to be adaptable. This gift of flexibility creates a "here and now" dynamic which also encourages and allows the adolescent to use his own unique and creative ways to deal with his grief experience. It is our goal to help the adolescent use resources that evolve from within, rather than from perceptions made by assuming adults. Spontaneity can inspire the adolescent to have the courage to grieve in ways that are intrinsic instead of extrinsic; in other words, from the inside, not the outside.

Patience

The caring adult must believe in the ability of the grieving adolescent to heal. Adults must be patient. In the case of a suicide where the adolescent discovered the deceased, the adolescent may need to tell the story many times. This can be healthy, as it helps the adolescent accept the reality of the tragedy emotionally as well as intellectually. The adult must remain patient and let the adolescent tell the story, even if they are tired of hearing it. Patience gives the adolescent the courage to grieve. It communicates the adult's desire to hang in there with the adolescent and to be willing to walk with them in this time of need. In other words, the adult's attitude about the desire to understand and belief in the ability of the adolescent to heal is demonstrated in word and deed. Patience demonstrates a commitment that instills trust, self-respect and hope for the grieving adolescent.

The caring adult must believe that they can make a positive difference in a troublesome situation. With the above characteristics, they facilitate healing as they become partners with the grieving adolescent through the grief journey.

Chapter
8

Advice for the Caring Adult
From Adolescents

Chapter Eight

Advice for the Caring Adult from Adolescents

This work would not be complete without input from the adolescents we are trying to serve. We compiled a list of suggestions for adults and peers from a past support group we facilitated. Their advice can be very helpful for caring adults and the grieving adolescent' friends as we attempt to guide and support them through these tough times. We split the group into four smaller groups. Their task was to give advice as to how we could better serve and support them as they go through the grief process. They developed a list of fourteen suggestions. Numbers 5, 6, and 7 are specifically for their friends, while the rest are for both adults and their friends:

1. ***"Mention our loved one who died by name."***

   What we believe our group was trying to communicate to us is to *personalize* their loss. When we personalize their loss, we validate their feelings. It is also comforting for the people to hear their deceased love one's name. Experts tell us it reassures the grieving person that their departed friend or family member will not be forgotten.

2. ***"Please don't be afraid to talk to us about the person who died. Don't pretend that he/she didn't exist."***

   The grieving teen, in his or her own time, desires to talk about the person who died. When acquaintances purposefully avoid this particular conversation, the grieving adolescent usually perceives this as indifference. Once indifference is perceived on the part of a close friend or adult, it becomes almost impossible for productive conversation that is so very critical for the healing process to occur.

3. ***"Use the words 'dead' 'died' 'death.'"***

   Adolescents tell us that when friends or adults use other words to describe the situation, they get the feeling the adult really doesn't want to address the difficult issues involved in a grief situation. We live in a death denying society; however, adolescents want to confide in adults who are willing to tackle the issues head on.

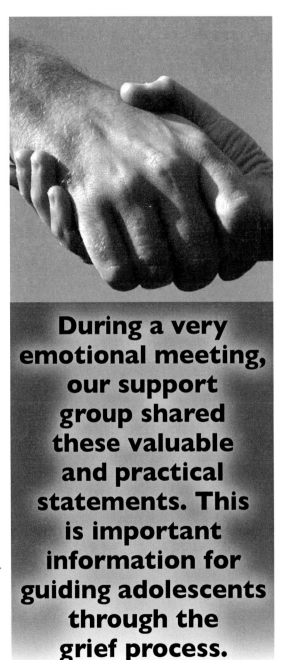

During a very emotional meeting, our support group shared these valuable and practical statements. This is important information for guiding adolescents through the grief process.

4. **"Be patient. If we cry, please understand.**
   If we make you feel uncomfortable, we don't mean to."

   We believe that this is the adolescent's plea to the caring adult to hang in there with him. We also believe that this plea reveals that young people want and need caring adults in their lives.

5. **"Call and visit. Please don't wait for us to call you."**

   When people suffer a significant loss in their lives, they become so overwhelmed, they forget to call for help or they don't have the energy to call. Grieving takes a great deal of energy causing an abnormal amount of fatigue. We believe the adolescents are asking people to be proactive in their approach with them.

6. **"If you see one of us sitting alone at church, in a restaurant,**
   or anywhere else, please offer to sit with us."

   This statement shows that the grief journey can be a lonely one indeed. The adult or friend in this situation may not even need to talk about the loss, but show genuine care for the grieving adolescent. By sitting next to him, the adult or friend acknowledges him. This acknowledgement can be more important than most people know.

7. **"If you call and ask us to join you at some function and we say no,**
   please call back for another time."

   The adolescent may not be able to make it for a number of reasons. The statement does show that they do want caring people in their lives. Our advice to the friend and/or adult is not to be too pushy, but do call back another time.

8. **"Please remember that the normal grief cycle lasts about 24 months.**
   In case of suicide, the grief cycle may last even longer."

   This statement was made in regard to the frustration of people putting time limits on them for their grieving process. Many teens reported to us that people (including adults) were saying, "Come on, snap out of it. It has already been one year." When adults understand the duration of the grief cycle, they can certainly be more patient and understanding of the adolescent.

9. **" 'Thinking of you' cards or notes on anniversaries of death,**
   Father's Day, Mother's Day, the dead person's birthday,
   or other memorable events, are greatly appreciated."

   The group wished to communicate that it is good to know that people care and remember. Great comfort comes to those who are grieving when people in their lives truly demonstrate that they care.

10. ***"If we vent our anger toward you, please forgive us."***

Although the anger may be vented towards the adult, the adult is not the cause. The young person does not mean anything personal, but at times must vent pent up anger and many times aims it at the nearest person willing to listen. The caring adult must not forget that by this statement, the adolescent is asking for forgiveness. Expect the anger, but try not to take it personally.

11. ***"Please don't tell us that you know how we feel."***

As stated before, when we tell people "I know how you feel," we are actually telling them that they cannot talk to us because they know we *don't know* how they feel. We also fail to validate their feelings when we use this inappropriate but often uttered statement. Remember, since grief is a unique experience for all, we can't possibly know how a person feels, even if we have suffered through a similar experience.

12. ***"Please don't tell us 'you are the man/woman of the house now; you have to take care of your mom/dad, siblings.'"*** (Teens whose parents died)

Let's put this in perspective. The grieving teen has just lost a parent to death. A "caring adult" has come to the funeral home during visitation, puts his arm around the grieving adolescent and gives him the "you're the man of the house now" talk. This can be a very cold and cruel thing to say to them at this particular time. The teen just lost a parent. He doesn't need any additional responsibilities heaped on him at this time, especially the heavy responsibility of caring for his household. The adolescent needs comfort at this time, not added responsibility.

13. ***"Please be happy with us when something good happens."***

We have already stated that "grief shared is grief decreased." Another key concept is "joy shared is joy *increased.*" To help increase joy that is initiated by the grieving adolescent is a great opportunity for the caring adult to develop rapport and is a great shot in the arm for the healing process to progress. The caring adult should not try to create this situation; it must come from the grieving adolescent (examples: passed driver's test, made the honor roll, won a contest or other noteworthy event). When it does come, don't miss it. Remember, *joy shared is joy increased.*

14. ***"Help us to laugh again."***

This statement reveals to us that the young person really wants to get better, to heal. Humor therapy can be very beneficial when it is used with discretion and in the appropriate situation. We feel that by making this statement, the grieving adolescent is asking the caring adult to give him hope. We can give the adolescent hope when we take the time to listen, encourage, share and care.

Chapter

9

Return to School

Chapter Nine

The Return to School

It is our belief that adolescents grieving the death of a classmate, close friend, or loved one should not be asked to continue with schoolwork as if nothing has happened. The work of grieving must take priority if the adolescent is to heal. Teachers should understand and even encourage this *temporary* shift in priorities. Important events such as prom or graduation may cause the bereaved adolescent to feel particularly sad because the friend or family member who died is not there to share the moment. This is normal not only a short time after the death, but also years later. We highly recommend that educators identify students impacted by such tragedy and make notes in their planners on dates that will be especially difficult for these grieving adolescents as a reminder to send them a "thinking of you" card or some other acknowledgement of care. There is no need to mention the tragedy in these cards as we guarantee the young person will be thinking about the tragic incident. Please use the ***"Thinking Of You" Information Sheet (p. 79)*** to help remember special dates and anniversaries for individual grieving students.

The School's Role

Classrooms for many teens serve as secondary or even substitute families. The dynamics of the classroom may be especially important when parents are so deep in grief that they are unable to provide their teen with much-needed attention. In these cases, adolescents lose not only the person who died but, in a sense, the surviving parent(s) as well. School personnel are frequently willing to assume the parental role, but most feel insecure about the possibility of saying or doing the wrong thing. The school should have a three-pronged goal in helping this adolescent:

1. Acknowledge the death honestly.

2. Allow classmates and staff to express feelings.

3. Offer an outlet for classmates and staff who desire to help.

Before the Student Returns

The following guidelines can be helpful for a teacher wishing to understand and support the grieving student. These guidelines should be reviewed after *any* death that will impact the adolescent in a tragic manner:

- Before the student returns to school, have the class send a card expressing sympathy to the student and his family.

- If possible, attend the visitation at the funeral home, funeral or memorial service. This sends a message of support to the adolescent.

- Discuss the student's return with the class. Emphasize that the adolescent has just experienced a great loss and will need a long time to adjust.

- Help the students think through how they will interact with their grieving classmate.

- Encourage them to act as normally as possible. Talk about helping the student feel part of the class, as he was before the tragedy.

- Help the student feel welcome, but don't make a big fuss.

The First Day Back

The return to school after the death of a loved one is an important first step for the grieving student. It signals a return (or an attempt to return) to a normal life. The teacher must provide structure and expectations regarding schoolwork but be flexible with regard to time for assignments to be completed. The first day back, the staff needs to help the student get settled. The guidance department should have some form of debriefing procedure for the adolescent to let him know people care and help him enlist people who he feels could help him through this difficult time.

The school staff should make sure the adolescent does not feel isolated from others. The counselor or teacher should *never* pressure him to talk but let him know that they care and are available to listen and help. The following is a list of suggestions which may provide additional help to the classroom teacher:

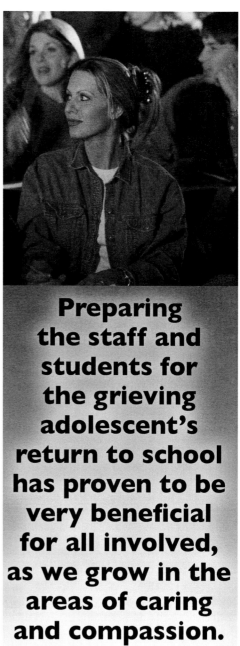

What *TO* Do

- Act as natural as possible. Don't be afraid to share your feelings about the loss. It is okay to shed a few tears with the grieving student. Avoid confusing statements such as "went away," "expired" or "went to sleep."

- Use the correct language (death, dead, died) with sensitivity. Listen and accept. Let the adolescent tell you what is bothering him or what is personally important to him. Be alert for uncharacteristic behaviors related to grief, such as truancy, lack of interest in school, anger toward classmates, teachers or administrators or physical manifestations such as frequent headaches, loss of weight, etc.

- Allow the young person to talk about the loss as much as needed. Do not impose your religious beliefs. Don't be afraid to make mistakes. Most of the time, when your heart is right, so will be your instincts. An error in judgment will not destroy an adolescent. Prolonged or abnormal grief behavior may signal a need to make a referral to the counseling department or a meeting with the teens's parent(s). Make sure he knows you care and are willing to help. Keep in touch with the family.

Preparing the staff and students for the grieving adolescent's return to school has proven to be very beneficial for all involved, as we grow in the areas of caring and compassion.

The following comments can help the grieving adolescent upon the return to school:

- "I am sorry that (<u>name</u>) died." (Rather than I'm sorry about what happened).

- "I cannot know how you feel, but I want to help you in any way I can."

- "I care about you."

- "Let's talk about what might make you feel more comfortable in class."

- "You may want to keep a journal to help you express your feelings."

- "If you feel like sharing any of your writing with me, I would like to read it."

- "I can see you are very sad."

- "I cannot know how you feel, but I also had a death in my family and I know how painful that loss was for me." *(Briefly share a personal story to help build trust.)*

What *NOT* To Do

To be on the safe side, we feel it important to list some common mistakes we have witnessed over the years by well-meaning teachers. The intent here is not to criticize, but to inform for the good of the adolescent.

- Don't avoid the student.

- Don't minimize the loss.

- Don't change the subject if the adolescent brings up the deceased.

- Don't tell them that the hurt will go away. No one knows how long the grief cycle will last.

- Don't tell the adolescent, "I know how you feel."

- Don't use clichés like, "We all have to die sometime," or "At least you knew it was coming," or "It definitely was God's will."

A very difficult problem in our culture is helping teens find their way following the death of a loved one. In many situations their questions and feelings are ignored. Communication about death is easier when adolescents feel they have permission to talk about the subject and believe that others really care about their feelings and are interested in their questions.

Chapter 10

Developing and Facilitating a Support Group

Chapter Ten
Developing and Facilitating a Support Group

Developing a Support Group

Support groups can be an appropriate and effective way to help grieving adolescents heal. They offer a safe place for them to do the work of mourning, to find encouragement, to reconcile their losses and to go on to find continued meaning in life and living. The formation and makeup of the group will depend heavily on the ability of the adult facilitator, the time he or she can invest and the support system in place in the school and community.

The Role of the Support Group

In developing a support group, it is of paramount importance that the group has clearly defined roles. The following list may help the caring adult as he attempts to develop such a group to:

- Offer a safe place for adolescents to do the work of mourning and encourage members to reconcile their losses and go on to find continued meaning in life and living.

- Counter the sense of isolation that many experience.

- Provide emotional, physical and spiritual support.

- Allow mourners to explore their many thoughts and feelings about grief in a way that helps them to be compassionate with themselves.

- Encourage adolescents to not only receive support and understanding, but also to provide the same for others.

- Offer opportunities to learn new ways of approaching problems.

- Provide a supportive environment that can revitalize the adolescent's zest for life.

As group members give and receive help, they feel less helpless and are able to discover new meaning in life. Feeling understood by peers brings down barriers between the grieving adolescent and the world outside.

Getting Started

Starting a support group can take a great deal of time and energy. The caring adult must evaluate carefully if he/she has the time to fully commit to such a task. One idea is to co-facilitate a group. This way, responsibilities and time commitments can be shared. It is always better when a group of compassionate people can share the workload and also bring a variety of creative ideas to the process. Listed below you will find suggestion to help you form a support group.

- ### *Decide on a group format*

   A "self-help" format or "social group" format? In choosing the format, the strength of the facilitator(s) and the personality of the group should be considered.

- ### *Find a meeting place*

   Obviously, the best place will be a comfortable, safe place appropriate for creating a supportive atmosphere, usually distraction free.

- ### *Establish the structure*

   Will it be "open-ended," meaning that the group members come and go depending on their needs? Or will it be "close-ended," meaning that the group will meet for a specific number of days or weeks?

- ### *Determine the length and frequency of meetings*

   We have been successful meeting one day a week for no longer than one hour.

- ### *Set the number of participants*

   The number of support group members will be related to the kind and quality of interaction the facilitator desires. When groups get too large, the sense of safety and freedom to express feelings diminishes for many people. For involved interaction, try to limit the group to no more than twelve persons.

- ### *Create Group Rules*

   Through establishing ground rules, you can create a safe place for adolescents to mourn. Ground rules are also important for the facilitator's role as leader. For example, should someone begin to verbally dominate the discussion, the facilitator intervenes by pointing out a ground rule that ensures members will have equal time to express themselves. It is important to discuss the rules at the first meeting and also give opportunity for the group members to have input and help develop some rules. This creates a sense of ownership on the part of the group members and gives them the feeling that their insights are important.

Sample Support Ground Rules

- Respect and accept both what you have in common with others and what is unique to you.
- Don't set a specific timetable for how long it should take you and others to heal.
- Feel free to talk about your grief. However, if someone in the group decides to listen without sharing, please respect his or her preference.
- Make every effort not to interrupt when someone else is speaking.
- Respect others' rights to confidentially. Do not use names of fellow participants in discussions outside the group.
- Allow each person equal time to express himself or herself.
- Avoid giving advice unless a group member specifically requests it.
- Recognize that thoughts and feelings are neither right nor wrong.
- If you feel pressured to talk but don't want to, say no. Your right to quiet contemplation will be respected by the group.
- If you wish to express anger, you must do so in an appropriate manner. No throwing chairs, punching walls, etc.

These rules should be posted at each meeting so all group members can see and read them. It is imperative that each group member knows and understands the rules. The group facilitator may wish to also quickly review these rules at the start of every meeting.

In dealing with confidentiality, the group facilitator should explain that there are times when they will break confidentiality, such as if a person threatens to harm himself or others. If confidentiality is broken by a group member, the group should be given the opportunity to discuss how it should be handled. The facilitator should remind the group that it is okay to get mad at this leak of confidentiality, but it is not okay to be mean. The group will also be instrumental, if given the opportunity, in establishing ground rules.

Facilitator Roles

The role of the facilitator is to literally "make easier" purposeful discussion about the grief journey of group members. The group facilitator needs to keep in mind that the purpose of the group is to create a safe place for adolescents to do the work of mourning in a way that allows them to reconcile the loss and find continued meaning in life and living.

Two important qualities in an effective group facilitator are flexibility and the ability to share authority. Being flexible is important because as the group evolves, some meetings may take a natural path without much direction from the facilitator. Sometimes the meeting plan, no matter how well organized, should be put aside if the group dynamic moves in a different direction.

The support group will be influenced by the unique personalities of the group members and the leadership style provided by the group facilitator. Some groups may move more quickly toward resolution. The most important thing the facilitator can do is evaluate the "safeness" of the group for adolescents to mourn, share and express their feelings. If the group is not moving forward, the facilitator must try to discern why the adolescents don't feel a sense of trust and safety. The support group can help the grieving adolescent move forward to develop a renewed sense of confidence, an ability to acknowledge the reality of the death, and the capacity to become involved with the activities of the living.

Typical Meeting Format

The following is an example of how a first meeting may go depending on the ability and style of the group facilitator. The facilitator should not feel tied to any format but always look to adjust meetings to the unique needs of the group members.

Set up chairs in a circle so all can have eye contact with each other

First Meeting Plan

1. Have group members share their name, the name and relationship of the person who died, and something positive that has happened in their lives. (*Celebration of Life*)

2. Facilitator explains purpose of the group.

3. Ground rules are shared, discussed, and the group is asked if additional rules are needed. If so, members give input.

4. Develop group motto – facilitator suggests a few, group members share ideas for the group motto. Vote taken, motto picked.

5. Brainstorm possible group activities related to motto.

6. "Thinking of you" information sheet filled out and handed to facilitator.

7. Dismiss with a short encouraging story (*Chicken Soup, Letters from the Heart, etc.*).

Definition of Key Terms

Celebration of Life

The group member briefly shares something positive and/or encouraging that has happened in his life. This can be recent or something that occurred a long time ago.

Group Motto

Motto chosen by group to solidify its purpose. Examples of a group motto are *"Remembering is Healthy," "Together We Stand," "Helping Each Other Grieve and Grow,"* etc.

"Thinking of You" Information Sheet

An information sheet filled out by group members and given to the facilitator so "thinking of you" cards can be sent to a group member on a particularly difficult day. (examples include anniversary of death, deceased person's birthday, Mothers Day, Fathers Day, or any other day or event during the year that is difficult for the grieving adolescent. (*See the **"Thinking of You" Fact Sheet**, p. 79*)

Once the group facilitator gets a feel for the needs of the group, discussion topics and group activities can be developed based on the needs of the group and the group members' willingness to take ownership in the discussions and activities.

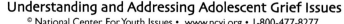

Meeting Topics of Discussion

We have found the following topics of discussion to be extremely beneficial to group members in helping them to better understand the grief journey:

1. *Explanation and discussion of the grief cycle*

   Granger Westberg, in his book "Good Grief" gives an easy to understand ten-step process. This may take two to three meetings to cover but is well worth the time.

2. *Specific Grief Issues*

   Discussed in smaller groups and a report is made to the group as a whole. (*See Specific Grief Issues, Fact or Fiction*, p. 82 -83)

3. *How to support each other*

   A whole group discussion identifying the difference between supporting and commiserating, and what people need and don't need when they are grieving.

4. *Common Triggers*

   What are they? Why do they come? What do they mean? How do we explain them to our friends so they won't feel awkward or like they said something that hurt us? (*See Common Triggers*, p. 84)

5. *Grief issues unique to adolescents* (*Please review Chapter 6 p. 45-47*)

Group Activities

It is very important that the group does more than discuss grief issues. Activities are great therapy for the grieving adolescent. Our most recent adolescent grief support group developed some of the following activities to match their motto "Remembering is Healthy":

1. *Memory Collage*

   Students can include pictures of them with their loved one at holidays, fun activities, as well as individual photos. They may include bits of memorabilia, (newspaper clippings, trophy ribbons, etc.) from their loved one as well. Have them present their collages to the whole group.

2. *Memory Pillows*

   This is the same concept as the collage. Presenting and sharing significant designs and their meanings was very therapeutic.

3. *Memory Garden*

   Group members designed, planted, and cared for a flower garden at our Historic Village in honor of their deceased loved ones. Local garden shops donated flowers and decorative rocks. The flower garden was the site of our ice cream socials during the summer months.

4. *Dedication and Memorial Journal Page*

   Have the members decorate a cover for a Memory Journal. Encourage them to include a photo of their loved one. Make copies of the **Dedication and Memorial Journal Page**, *(p. 80-81)* and have them write their thoughts and memories of their loved one to give them comfort during the grieving process.

Additional Points

Parental permission is a good idea for adolescents who wish to participate in the support group. Possible parent dissent could cause conflicts, including legal problems. A ***Parental Permission Form (p. 86)*** is provided which you may copy, modify, and use. *****Make sure that you include a letter stating the purpose, intended outcomes, meeting times, (if they are after regular school hours) and any other details that parents might need to know about your group***.

Support groups are not a good fit for everyone. We have assisted grieving adolescents who worked through their grief without a support group. Some may feel more comfortable sharing on an individual basis. The caring adult should never insist that the grieving teen join a support group. In dealing with grief, what works for one usually doesn't work for all.

Support groups for adolescents should have a closing phase. The closing date should be established before the first meeting occurs. Studies reveal that if the group goes on indefinitely, staleness usually occurs, countering the growth and healing that has taken place. If an adolescent has not progressed, make arrangements to meet him one on one or include him in a future group. In the closing phase, the group facilitator's responsibilities include:

- Acknowledge what growth needs yet to occur.
- Reinforce positive changes and growth.
- Assist adolescents in setting realistic goals for the future.
- Assist adolescents in applying specific skills in everyday life.
- Provide closure individually as well as for the group.

A support group's main goal is not to give therapy, but to give the adolescent a supportive environment. In misery, people need someone to hold their hand as they walk through it. The effective support group lets its members be who they are in a familiar environment and doesn't solve problems of the past, but helps young people deal with them.

We don't want to leave you with the impression that all caring adults who are working with grieving adolescents should form a support group. We just wish to provide the caring adult with some structure in the event he feels the need to develop one.

In Review

In working with the grieving adolescent, the caring adult must remember that he is responsible *to* the adolescent, not *for* the adolescent. The adult must be careful not to get so involved in the emotions of the situation that clear judgments are inhibited. It is also emotionally unhealthy for anyone to be so involved that they bring the young person's problems into their personal world.

The caring adult will be more effective if he enters into the teen's feelings without having a need to change those feelings. Feelings are very hard to change, and trying to change them can be very frustrating for the adult. The adolescent may see the adult who tried to change his feelings as a threat. Dealing with feelings and trying to change them are two different concepts. The caring adult should know the difference between the two.

Also important to keep in mind is that while adolescents are able to experience feelings similar to adults, their thought processes are quite different. The lack of life experiences because of their youth usually will prevent them from seeing things from an adult perspective. Therefore, the caring adult must remember to enter the adolescent's world first and counsel second. The adult needs to remember how they were themselves as a young, naive teen and respond accordingly to the student. In this regard, the caring adult will earn the trust and respect needed to be effective and helpful to the grieving adolescent.

Grieving adolescents use behaviors (regressive, aggressive, explosive, among many) to teach adults about underlying needs (security, trust or encouragement). The caring adult must learn what those unmet needs are and help the adolescent get those needs met. However, remember that we cannot fix the problem but, in most cases, we believe that adults can meet the needs of the grieving adolescent.

Helping the adolescent embrace memories of the loved one or close friend who died will help him discover hope for a new tomorrow. It can be very comforting for the grieving adolescent to focus on fond memories, reminding him that no one can take these loving memories away. These cherished recollections can also give the grieving adolescent a deeper appreciation for life and his remaining loved ones. This deeper appreciation will help when the adolescent becomes depressed as he goes through the grief process. *(See **Dedication and Memorial Journal Page**, p. 80-81)*

It is a noble task. Helping the adolescent work toward reconciliation will encourage him to develop a renewed sense of energy and confidence. Fully acknowledging the reality of the death will increase their capacity to become re-involved in the activities of living. A noble task indeed!

Appendix

"Thinking of You" Information Sheet

Your Name _____

Name of Deceased _____

Date of Death _____

Parent _____ *Sibling* _____ *Grandparent* _____

Godparent _____ *Close Friend* _____ *Aunt/Uncle* _____ *Significant Person* _____

Deceased's Birthday _____

Parents Wedding Anniversary _____

Your Birthday _____

Days that are especially difficult for you during the year:

_____

_____

_____

_____

_____

_____

Dedication and Memorial Journal Page

This page is dedicated to the memory of; ————————————————————————
name and relationship

_____

Things I remember about you that make me smile are;

_____

_____

_____

_____

_____

_____

_____

_____

_____

_____

_____

Things I find especially hard or painful to remember are;

_____

_____

_____

_____

_____

_____

_____

_____

_____

_____

_____

_____

_____

Days that might be especially difficult for me without you here are: *(anniversaries, birthdays, holidays, etc.)*

_____
_____
_____
_____

If I could write you a letter I would say;

_____
_____
_____
_____
_____
_____
_____
_____
_____
_____
_____
_____
_____
_____
_____
_____

Things I want to do to remember our good times together are; *(memory quilt, balloon release, etc.)*

_____
_____
_____
_____
_____

Though I know I will miss you deeply, _____
relationship (exp. my friend, my brother, my mother, etc.)

I know I will cherish the memories we had together. I am better for having loved you.
I will go on remembering you. Rest in Peace.

_____
your name

Specific Grief Issues *Fact or Fiction?*

Directions – Split the group into smaller groups and have them answer the following items *fact* or *fiction*. Each group is to have a recorder and a reporter to share thoughts with the whole group concerning their assigned items. (I assigned at least three items to each small group)

1. Bereaved people need only to express their feelings and they will resolve their grief:

     a. _____Fact b. _____ Fiction

2. Expressing feelings that are intense is the same as losing control:

     a. _____Fact b. _____Fiction

3. It is better to tell bereaved people to "be brave" and "keep a stiff upper lip" because they will not have to experience as much pain:

     a. _____Fact b. _____Fiction

4. There is no such person as a grief expert:

     a. _____Fact b. _____Fiction

5. When grief is resolved, it never comes up again:

     a. _____Fact b. _____Fiction

6. Grief always declines over time in a steadily decreasing fashion:

     a. _____Fact b. _____Fiction

7. You will eventually be the same over time after the death of a loved one:

     a. _____Fact b. _____Fiction

8. Grief will affect you psychologically, but in no other way:

     a. _____Fact b. _____Fiction

9. After the death of a loved one, there is something wrong if you do not always feel close to your friends and family, since you should be happy you still have them:

     a. _____Fact b. _____Fiction

10. All losses due to death are basically the same:

     a. _____Fact b. _____Fiction

11. All bereaved people grieve in the same way:

     a. _____Fact b. _____Fiction

12. You will have no relationship with your loved one after his/her death:

     a. _____Fact b. _____Fiction

13. It is better to put painful things out of your mind:

     a. _____Fact b. _____Fiction

14. You should not think about your deceased loved one at anniversaries or holidays because it will make you feel sad:

     a. _____Fact b. _____Fiction

15. Once your loved one has died, it is best to put them in the past and move on with your life:

     a. _____Fact b. _____Fiction

Note: The group facilitator may selectively choose the items to be discussed that best fit the group's needs. Also, the facilitator can mix and match items and use them over the course of the group meetings.

Common Triggers

For a grieving person, a "trigger" happens when all of a sudden, without warning, the grieving person becomes overwhelmed with sadness many times causing an outward expression of emotion such as a sudden cry. A song, a picture, or remembering a past experience may "trigger" the emotional response. The following is an example of how the grief support group facilitator might address the issue:

1. Define the term "trigger."

2. Share a time in your life that you (facilitator) or someone you know experienced a trigger.

3. Ask if anyone in the group wished to share a time when they had experienced an emotional trigger.

4. Discuss what may bring them on.

5. Stress that triggers are a normal part of the grief process. All grieving people do not experience them, but many do.

6. What problems may arise if one of us has a trigger in the midst of our friends?"

7. Why is it important (when you are able) to explain to your friends that this is a normal part of the grief process?

8. Should we apologize for making our friends uncomfortable if we have a trigger? Why or why not?

9. Stress that triggers are just a testimony that you deeply loved and miss your deceased loved one.

10. End with a celebration of life.

Fundamental Steps for Grief Survival
Helpful Hints for Caring Adults for Grieving Adolescents

1. Recognize the loss – for a while you are numb. It has happened. Try not to avoid it.

2. Bear with the pain. You are hurting, admit it. To feel pain after a loss such as yours, is normal.

3. You are a beautiful, worthwhile person – you are much more than the emotional wound you are presently feeling.

4. Give yourself time to heal – believe that you will heal.

5. Heal at your own pace. Never compare yourself to another grieving person.

6. Be gentle with yourself . You have suffered an emotional wound so treat yourself with care.

7. Good eating habits are important.

8. Suicidal thoughts may occur. They are a symptom of pain. If you feel that they are getting out of control, ***SEEK HELP AT ONCE!!!***

9. It is okay to feel anger. Most everyone gets angry at the loss of a loved one. Channel your anger wisely.

10. Give yourself praise. You are a deeper person with a wider perspective on life.

11. Expect relapses. There will always be certain things that trigger sadness again. This is normal.

12. Crying can be a cleansing and healthy release.

Note: The above is a short list. We encourage you to add to this list as you work with grieving adolescents.

Parental Release Form

I _____, the parent of _____

      ☐   **DO** give my permission for my child to participate

      ☐   **DO NOT** give my permission for my child to participate

      in a Grief Support Group, established by _____.

Parents/Guardians signature _____

Principal signature _____

                       Date: _____

cc: Principal's Confidential File/Superintendent

Understanding and Addressing Adolescent Grief Issues
© National Center For Youth Issues • www.ncyi.org • 1-800-477-8277
Please refer to page 4 for duplication information

References

Breier, Alan. "Early Parental Loss and Development of Adult Psychopathology." Archives of General Psychology 45 (1988): 987-993

Furman, Erna. "A Child's Parent Dies." Cambridge, Mass., 1974, Yale University press

Osterweis, Marian, Solomon, Fredric, and Green, Morris. "Bereavement: Reactions, Consequences, and Care." Washington, DC: National Academy Press, 1984.

Bryan, Mellonie, "Lifelines." Bantam Books, 1983.

Cohn, Janice. "I had a friend Named Peter." Morrow, 1987.

Scneidman, Edwin. "The Suicidal Mind." Oxford University Press, N.Y., N.Y.

Gordon, S. "When Living Hurts." Dell Books, Feb. 1989, N.Y., N.Y.

Smolin, C. and Guinan, J. "Healing After the Suicide of a Loved One." Simon and Schuster, 1993, N.Y., N.Y.

Michigan Association of Suicidology, Oct. 1997 Newsletter, Lansing, MI

National Center for Health Statistics Centers for Disease Control and Prevention. 1997, Atlanta, GA

Wolfelt, Alan. "Healing the Bereaved Child." Companion Press, 1996, Fort Collins, CO.

Bronson, Howard. "Early Winter: Learning to Live, Love and Laugh Again After a Painful Loss." A Bestsell Book, 1976, Sandwich, MA

National Center for Health Statistics, Monthly Vital Statistics Report, 45(3, suppl.) 2001

Kushner, Harold. "When Bad Things Happen to Good People." Avon Books, 1981

References Continued

Schneider, John, "Finding My Way." Seasons press, Colfax, WI 1994.

Rosenberg, Larry. "Living in the Light of Death." Shambhala Publications, Inc., Boston, Mass. 2,000.

Granello, Darcy, and Granello, Paul. "Suicide: An Essential Guide for Helping Professionals and educators." Pearson Education Inc. 2007

Canfield, Jack, Hansen, Mark Victor. "Chicken Soup for the Grieving Soul." Health Communications Inc. 2003

Manning, Doug. "Don't Take My Grief Away, Harper & Row, 1984

McEvoy & McEvoy. "Preventing Youth Suicide: A Handbook for Educators and Human Service Professionals." Learning Publications. 1984.

Westberg, Granger. "Good Grief." Fortress Press. 1962

Templer & Lonette. Research papers: "Death Anxiety." Wash. DC. 1986

VanDexter, Mark. "Loss and Anticipatory Grief." Lexington Books, Lexington, Mass. 1986

McIntrye, Osterweiss, Marian. "Bereavement: Reactions, Consequences, and Care." Institute of Medicine: Committee for the study of Health Consequences of Stress and Bereavement, National Academy Press, Washington, DC 1984.

Matter & Matter, "Child and Adolescent Grief." Social Work Journal, 1982.